THE EMOTIONAL DIVORCE

Bishop D. G. Hood

Dedication

This book is dedicated to every couple that has endured the storms of challenge in their marriage and yet remains resolute in their commitment to one another and the marital bond. For without your experiences this book would be a vain and fruitless effort. Your commitment and perseverance authenticate the message of this book and validate the process of overcoming The Emotional Divorce.

1st Edition

Cover design by Mcube Graphic Design.
Interior book design by PegDuVal-Art.

Printed in the United States of America.

New Life Worship Center Ministries International
Ft. Lauderdale, FL

Acknowledgements

I would like to thank my wife, Angela, for your endless motivation and encouragement. Your persistence in urging me to complete this book was not in vain. Thank you, babe!

To my spiritual sons and daughters at New Life Worship Center and the Enrichment Center Ministries, I thank God for allowing me the privilege of leading such a wonderful group of people.

To everyone who will read this book, thank you for allowing me to share the awesome experiences that make ministry such an important part of my life. May your lives and marriages forever be enriched and blessed.

Thank you.

Bishop D. G. Hood

Chapter 1

THE EMOTIONAL DIVORCE

When Alissa and Steven met twenty years ago it wasn't exactly love at first sight; it was more like infatuation. Within a matter of months both quickly realized that there seemed to be a deeper connection beyond mere college sweethearts. Before long, they had developed a deep, intimate relationship. To everyone on the outside looking in the relationship seemed perfect and essentially it was. While they connected on an emotional and physical level there was always a white elephant in the room. Alissa was a Christian and Steven really wanted very little to do with God.

Steve had grown up in the Christian faith but when his mother passed away his sophomore year of high school, he turned his back on God and denied his faith. He didn't care that Alissa remained steadfast in her faith but he never made any promises to change. He wasn't antagonistic towards Alissa and he wasn't encouraging either. Although sometimes he didn't always understand why Alissa was away so often at various church events, the fact that it was important to her was enough reason to back off and let her be.

When Alissa married Steven she did so on good faith, believing that she could win him over to God's side if he could only see that religion was a delight and not a duty. She paid careful attention to keep negative comments about church members to herself and tried to paint a positive picture of spiritual things. No matter how hard she tried, Alissa simply couldn't get Steven to even attend church. He just wouldn't budge. Anytime she broached the subject he would erupt in anger, the old scars of the past breaking open once again to fresh wounds of spiritual pain. He didn't bother her about her faith, he would say, and therefore he wanted the ambivalence reciprocated.

One thing led to another and eventually weeks turned into months that turned into years of Alissa doing her "spiritual thing" and Steven finding other things to occupy his time while she was away at various church functions. He never fussed about her taking the children along but always made it clear that church was "not his thing" no matter how hard she begged him to come. Even on Easter and Christmas he simply refused to acquiesce. Eventually their son became just like Steven and slowly Alissa found herself walking into the church door alone, her daughter sometimes trailing behind her.

Slowly through the years, Alissa found that she had less and less to talk to Steven about but more and more to argue about. She felt as if she had an entirely different life at church that her husband wanted nothing to do with. Most of her church friends had never even met Steven at all and she was tired of people saying, "I'm praying for you." It was embarrassing, it was tiring and, above all, it was lonely. The longer they were married, the chasm of spiritual disconnection grew wider and wider until eventually the space separating them seemed insurmountable.

■ ■ ■

What Alissa and Steven were facing was an emotional divorce. Yes, they were still married on paper, sleeping in the same bed at night and remaining sexually faithful to their partner, but emotionally, they were drifting further and further apart. Their marriage had spiraled to the point of spiritual disconnection, resulting in an emotional separation that had become their new reality. They felt as if they were living with a stranger and a single question permeated their thoughts: how did things become so messed up?

The emotional divorce begins when the marital bond suffers from an emotional, physical or spiritual disconnection. Couples can no longer function and communicate on a level that is healthy. They begin the process of isolating and limiting their interactions, creating an atmosphere of tension in the home. I have seen this over and over in couples that find themselves alone after years of child rearing are over and unhealthy patterns were never addressed.

Although couples often remain together in the home and even remain sexually involved during this stage of the emotional divorce they begin to function as individuals not a couple. They begin to have different hobbies, interests and groups of friends that have little, if anything, to do with one another. Their circles of influence stop colliding at all until eventually it is almost as if they are two strangers sharing a lease on an apartment rather than a husband and wife who are sharing an intimately connected spiritual life.

■ ■ ■

Consider the story of Jackie and Dan. The character quality that Dan most admired in Jackie would ultimately be what drove them apart: her work ethic. Dan had never met a woman who was as driven and worked as hard as Jackie. She could surpass any man he knew on workplace faithfulness and, as predicted, over the years she rose through the ranks of her company to become a vice-president.

The only problem was that Jackie's drive often left her family in the dust. Dan was a public school teacher and while his job was important it failed to bring in the income needed to raise their four children. Jackie's career was literally what kept food on the table, money in their retirement funds and paid for the kids various sports and activities. Most days it seemed like the family saw more of Jackie's money then they saw of her.

Jackie was unwilling to let go of her career and Dan was unwilling to give up the lifestyle the family had become accustomed to and so love and happiness were sacrificed for a fat paycheck that seemingly gave them everything that had dreamed of when they were just starting out years ago.

These days, however, if they saw if each other at all it was in between business trips and parent teacher conferences. Too often they were sacrificing date nights to simply hang out with friends from work or school. The small steps that they had taken away from each other over the years had now become a huge leap away from physical, emotional and spiritual intimacy. They may share the same last name but in all practicality they were nowhere near what a husband and wife should be.

■ ■ ■

The small steps that a couple takes away from each other in physical, emotional and spiritual intimacy can often be hard to diagnose. So many times it begins with something as simple and innocent as a decrease in their normal level of dialogue. Conversations become vague or limited to areas that cannot be avoided such as children and mutual financial obligations. A couple finds that apart from the humdrum musings of daily life, they have very few points of connection. In short, they simply stop trying to communicate with each other and rely on friends and family to fill this relational gap in their lives.

As the dialogue decreases the disconnection increases resulting in the couple closing their spirits towards one another. It becomes impossible to sustain any type of intimate relationship when the communication lines, both spoken and unspoken, are subconsciously shut down. They live in the same house, share the same bed, eat the same food and watch the same shows on television yet their realities could not be lived farther apart from one another.

It's at this point that their reasons for remaining in the marriage shift from their love for one another to the people and things that surround their lives. A young mother may want to leave her husband but for the sake of the children she stays. Without any means to financially support herself she feels stuck, promising herself that one day when she is financially ready she will walk away, but that day never seems to come. Others will stay in an emotionless marriage because they have financial assets they can't afford to lose. They are growing older and financial planning comes into the picture and suddenly things such as the house become too expensive to sacrifice for marital happiness.

Still others, and perhaps this is the most common reason, stay in an emotionless marriage because they are unable to face the social stigma of getting a divorce. They are afraid of the way others will look at them, including their friends at church, if they pursue a final end to their marriage. For someone in this situation, the power of other people's opinions is strong enough that they become paralyzed in an unhealthy marriage.

Whatever the reason may be, a couple enters the stage of existing or merely surviving in the relationship. They are no longer trying to thrive and live life to the fullest with their spouse as the exchange process by which the couple both gives and takes through mutual compromises is damaged and disengaged. Therefore, there is no longer the establishment of an enduring loving marital bond but a relationship that is on spiritual life support.

For many of you, it may seem like I am describing your daily reality. Sadly, you could write yourself into this book, word-for-word, as you realize that what you have been afraid to confront for years in your marriage is the truth: you are in the midst of an emotional divorce.

For others, perhaps you are reading this book because someone you love is experiencing an emotional divorce. It may be a parent, a close friend or spiritual advisor that you can see is slowly giving up on their marriage. The sadness and confusion you are experiencing through their dilapidated marriage is enough to make you want to understand and, hopefully, avoid the same mistakes.

Whatever your reason for reading this book, you are not alone.

Marriages in the United States are weaker than they have ever been. According to the organization Planning Family, 59% of minor children in the U.S. live in single parent homes.[1] It is also projected that 45% to 50% of first marriages will end in divorce. The number jumps even higher for second and third marriages.[2] If this number keeps rising, then eventually more than half of the men and women in America will not even have a healthy marriage pattern from their parents to model their own marriage upon. The stakes are too high to allow this to continue.

During my years of marital counseling as a pastor I have witnessed many couples that have decided to end their marriages after suffering a breakdown of the marital bond because of the emotional divorce. The question that I always ask is simple: how did you get to this place? How can two people who have shared so much of their lives together simply disconnect and disengage their love for one another? After listening to dozens of couples, including fellow pastors of failed marriages, I have identified the following factors that contribute to their condition:

---

[1] http://www.planningfamily.com/parents/single-parent/single-parents-the-truth-behind-cultural-stigmas/
[2] http://www.divorcestatistics.org/

- They fail to see their mate the way that God sees him/her.

- They have never learned how to resolve conflict in a healthy way.

- They have never improved the way they communicate with each other.

- They placed more emphasis on emotional love over covenantal love.

- They had conflicting views on finances that were never resolved.

It is a little known fact that how you see your mate will determine how you treat your mate. Over and over again I have seen couples come to me for marriage counseling that have chosen to only focus on the negative aspects of their partner. Either he doesn't help out enough around the house or she doesn't appreciate the hard day of work he puts in. Either she doesn't keep the house clean enough or he can't keep steady employment. Oftentimes the couple has to sit and think long and hard to finding one positive thing about their spouse. For these couples, the glass is more than half empty; it's ugly, beaten and cracked to the point of uselessness!

■ ■ ■

I remember several years ago while experiencing difficulties in my marriage that I began to focus on everything that I didn't like about my relationship with my wife. As we continued to endure our marital issues I began to form a negative perception of my wife. Everything that I disliked about her became magnified in my spirit. I allowed my spirit to spiral to the point of emotional separation and began to shut my wife out of my life. We went to church together and slept in the same bed together while being emotionally and spiritually divorced. I allowed my perception of my wife to create anger and frustration in my spirit.

One day while mowing the lawn God spoke to me and gave me a revelation that saved my marriage. He said to me, "Be careful of how you see your wife because how you see her is how you will treat her." I sat on my lawn mower in utter brokenness over the image of my wife that I allowed my sin and selfishness to create. The truth of God hit me right in the gut.

I had begun to disconnect from my wife emotionally and spiritually because I began to deal with her based on how I was seeing her. I saw her as a combatant because of the continual conflict in our marriage. We were no longer on the same side; we were now enemies and I drew the lines each and every day in my household, forcing us to each take opposing sides.

I didn't like her attitude so I gave her my attitude; my frustrations resulted in me treating her like a complaining, loud, frustrating woman that lived in the house with me. My faults and failures looked like roses when I compared myself next to her because I had created a false image of who my wife truly was on the inside. I had forgotten to see the potential in my spouse, just as God saw the potential in me.

From that day forward, I began to consciously focus on the positive and not the seemingly endless list of negative, nagging characteristics of my spouse. I began to compliment her and affirm the aspects about her character that drew me into a loving relationship so many years ago. In essence, I began to court my wife once again, learning how to love her as if we were in the beginning stages of a dating relationship. Just like a teenage boy who bends over backwards to open the door for his beloved, I made it my business to make my wife's positive aspects shine.

As I began to change how I saw my wife I noticed that my frustrations began to dissipate. I was no longer angry over every little thing she said and did that I disagreed with. In all honestly,

I found less and less to disagree with her about! My dialogue became less vague and I found that the woman that I fell in love with was still there under the mountain of frustrations that I felt in my heart. I had simply stopped looking.

■ ■ ■

Keeping the right perspective of your spouse is vital to the health and growth of your marital bond because how you see your mate is how you'll treat your mate. This ultimately affects all other areas of discord in marriage that lead to an emotional divorce including conflict, communication, love and money. As soon as you fail to see your spouse the way that God sees them, you've opened a Pandora's box of marital problems.

When God looks at your spouse, and you for that matter, He does not see a problem waiting to be fixed or an argument waiting to explode. Over and over again in the New Testament when Jesus looked on the crowds of people surrounding Him he did not react negatively. Actually, quite the opposite happened:

> *And Jesus, when He came out, saw a*
> *great multitude and was moved with*
> *compassion for them, because they were*
> *like sheep not having a shepherd. So*
> *He began to teach them many things.*[3]

It was the compassion of Christ that allowed Him to look upon the multitudes of men and women, no doubt constantly coming to Him to meet their spiritual and physical needs, and see them as beautiful, not burdensome. Perhaps it is time for you to reclaim a God-centered view of your spouse.

When you decide to see your spouse as God sees them, you are allowing yourself to consider the possibility of who your spouse could be if given the right support, love, help and opportunities.

3 Mark 6:34

You are ultimately seeing the potential of your spouse and looking beyond current situations and attitudes. This can be one of the hardest things to do because it is ultimately denying your needs and wants and focusing on the needs and wants of someone else. It is, however, the first step to healing your marriage relationship.

When the Apostle Paul was addressing his letter to the church at Philippi, he began it by saying:

> *I thank my God upon every*
> *remembrance of you, always in every*
> *prayer of mine making request for*
> *you all with joy, for your fellowship*
> *in the gospel from the first day*
> *until now, being confident of this*
> *very thing, that He who has begun*
> *a good work in you will complete*
> *it until the day of Jesus Christ;*[4]

Imaging the healing that could occur if you take the words of Paul and apply them to the way that you see your spouse. Imagine with each and every thought that you have of your spouse, you are quick to thank God for placing him or her in your life. Imagine the power that would come from believing that God has begun a good work in your spouse and the reason they aren't perfect is because God is not done yet! Just as He is still grooming and creating you to be the person He has destined for you to become, He is also working the same miracle in your spouse.

There is an old children's song with a simple chorus that goes:

> *He's still working on me*
> *To make me what I ought to be*

4 Galatians 1:3-6

It took him just a week to
make the moon and stars
The sun and the earth and
Jupiter and mars
How loving and patient he must be
He's still working on me.

The words are simple yet it does not give a simplistic message. The reality is that God is still working in each and every one of us to make us into the man or woman of God that He has ordained that we become. When we lash out at our spouse and focus on the unfinished product, we are waging an unfair war. If God is still working a good work in our mate then we must be patient and help our mate through the refiner's fire rather than hinder God's work by constant bickering and negativity.

When I got off of my lawn mower that summer day, it was not an instantaneous change on my part. I did not miraculously begin to treat my wife 100% perfectly. What I did do was make a conscious decision to change my thoughts. I told myself that I would no longer allow negative thoughts about my wife to permeate my brain. Instead, I would try my hardest to replace each negative thought with a focus on her strengths.

It is possible for an emotional divorce to change course and move towards marital health. If you are in this situation, just as God has not given up on you, it is not time for you to give up on your marriage. Take a step back and try your hardest to view your spouse in view of God and in view of the gospel. Allow God to change your perspective as you take the first step down the road of healing a broken relationship.

Chapter 2

RESOLVING CONFLICT
IN YOUR MARRIAGE

Tyler and Rebecca met in college and had a fairly stable, easygoing dating relationship. Similar interests made the courtship phase of their relationship fun and exciting and they experienced few, if any, arguments during the time leading up to their marriage. They really were simply a happy couple that got married without reservations that they would have a great marriage.

But then something happened the first few months into their marriage: they had their first *real* argument. They couldn't remember what it was about but they could certainly remember what happened. Tyler exploded into Rebecca and Rebecca retreated into a corner, tears welling up in her eyes, cowering like a frightened little animal. The effects of that first argument were devastating for learning how to resolve conflict in their marriage.

After that, Tyler kept anything to himself that might cause Rebecca even the smallest pain. He just couldn't bear to see his wife react that way again. He didn't want to cause her pain and if arguing caused her pain then he would learn to simply get over anything that bothered him in the marriage and "take one for the team". The only problem, however, was that Tyler found himself getting more and more frustrated at Rebecca refusing to confront any conflict in their marriage. As hard as he tried not to, his anger would boil over and erupt every few months. He would suppress it once again, often over flowers and chocolates for Rebecca.

By the time the couple came in for marital counseling they had experienced years of unhealthy conflict resolution. The behavior that Tyler first viewed as sensitive and sweet in Rebecca he was now beginning to see as manipulative. After all if you cried hard enough every time someone yelled at you they were bound to give in to whatever it was you wanted to make you happy.

In the eyes of Rebecca, it wasn't the conflict itself that bothered her, but the way that Tyler would simply rush into the conflict, all guns blazing, yelling without any direction or control. There was no calmness to the way he expressed his anger. When Tyler yelled, Rebecca shut down.

Through a series of discussions they started to reveal their own personal history of how they handled personal conflict prior to their marriage. It began to be evident that Tyler and Rebecca were coming at the issue of conflict management from two very different perspectives.

Rebecca grew up in a quiet, more subdued family than Tyler. When her parents argued it was always done in a calm, non-emotional manner. Both parties voiced their concerns and then moved on with things. She only remembered her parents arguing over extremely significant issues in their marriage, not squabbling over the every day little annoyances.

Tyler grew up in a loud, get-in-your-face family. Everybody was in each other business all the time and that made for some pretty explosive family reunions! In his opinion, you yelled to get something off of your chest and then you forgot about it. Sometimes it just felt good to yell. The two quickly realized they needed to find a common ground or their marriage wasn't going to last.

■ ■ ■

The initial and most important step to resolving conflict in your marriage is reflecting on how your parents modeled conflict management in the home in which you were raised. Chances are when you begin to uncover both the unhealthy and healthy ways that your mother and father duked it out at home, you'll see traces of both in your own conflict management style.

To help you work through how you acquired your personal conflict style, spend some time thinking through the following list of questions:

- When my parents argued, what was their physical posture?
- When my parents argued, who usually won? Was it even about winning?
- Did my parents argument style result in explosive anger or quiet, hushed discussions?
- Was conflict ever resolved in my parent's marriage? Did my parents yell and then walk away or force themselves to sit down and deal with the conflict?
- Who instigated the arguments, mom or dad?

Once you've allowed yourself time to really think through the answers to those questions, ask the same questions of your marriage. When you and your spouse argue is it about winning an argument in your mind or solving a disagreement? Do you tend to take on a defensive posture or, like Rebecca, find yourself cowering in the corner? Do you feel like you ever really resolve conflict or does it just result in one or both parties insincerely apologizing? Are you afraid of conflict?

Hopefully you are beginning to see patterns, both good and bad, in the inherited conflict management style you have acquired. Without even thinking about it, you simply adorn whatever argument style you are comfortable with and know. When the fists come out, you simply slip on the boxing gloves of your parents unconsciously, often catching your spouse off guard with your behavior. Conflict management, more than any other area of marriage, is where you most clearly realize that you are two individuals joining with the baggage of both families, who come together with two very different backgrounds.

Because insincere and hurtful things are often said in the heat of the moment during an argument, it can leave couples feeling isolated and alone, thinking that things will only get worse, not better. The good news is that it is possible for couples to overcome unhealthy conflict management styles and see a mediocre marriage transform into a great, healthy bond.

For the remainder of the chapter, I am going to expound on ten things to keep in mind to help you quickly resolve conflict in your marriage. If you share these tips with your spouse and both of you are willing to incorporate them into your marriage, then you are moving in a direction of marital health. Just as building a new home from scratch takes months of preparation, planning and hard work, so, too, healing a marriage is not going to be an overnight transformation. Don't expect your next argument to be perfect and, when it isn't, don't give up on these ten principles. Keep working and integrating these tips into your marriage and you'll eventually reap the rewards.

1. Be willing to listen to your spouse without feeling that you must defend yourself.

Many times in an argument the person with the loudest voice wins! This is especially true in marriages where one of the spouses is very soft spoken. Avoid the temptation of constantly interjecting while your spouse is talking. If your spouse never feels like they are able to fully complete a thought in the argument without being interrupted, then you simply must learn how to be quiet.

On the other hand, if you are the one that feels dominated by your spouse's interjections, then you may need a confidence booster. Believe that what you have to say is valuable to not just this conflict but also to the marriage as a whole. It takes both spouses working together to make a healthy marriage and if you are the one that's constantly in the background then perhaps it's time to discover the voice that God gave you to increase your contribution.

It is easy to get lost in a marriage and forget what you were like prior to the I do's. Each of you was an independent thinker who had dreams, goals and a future that you were working towards. Try very hard not to let one partner dominate the other.

2. Give your spouse your full attention while they are expressing their feelings.

When you and your spouse sit down to talk through a situation, minimize each and every distraction. Turn the cell phones off, wait until the children are taking a nap and press the power button on the TV remote! It is impossible to offer validation of your spouse with one eye on the basketball game, your fingers answering a work text or trying desperately to hush a screaming baby!

In the same way that you need to create a quiet environment to offer full attention to your spouse, it might also be a good idea to put off bringing an argument to the table until the timing is right. Confronting a spouse the moment they walk in the door from a long day's work or in the middle of a temper tantrum being thrown by a toddler is not an ideal time to discuss anything that may be difficult in a marriage. Just as the situation needs to be free from distractions, it also needs to happen in a relatively calm environment.

3. Keep your heart and spirit open and receptive. Don't shut down on your spouse.

Arguments, by their very definition, bring up issues that can be difficult to accept. Oftentimes when you are confronted with something that you are doing wrong or a character quality that is lacking and needs to be addressed, your defense mechanisms click on. When you feel attacked, the easiest response is to point out that the other person is no angel. Sure, you may have issues, but you could also sit and list the issues of your spouse, right?

Learning how to deal with conflict means that you begin to accept that you have weaknesses and sinful patterns that are hurting your marriage. Keep your heart and spirit open to the fact that perhaps you are not as perfect as you perceive. When your spouse is genuinely and honestly sharing about the things that hurt him or her, don't shut down and shut out your spouse.

Be sensitive to your posture during a conflict. Your spouse will be looking and noticing any body language that seems confrontational or defensive. Something as simple as uncrossing your arms can convey that you are unguarded and open to working through the conflict.

4. Listen to resolve the conflict not to respond or reply to their statements.

For too many men and women when they argue with their spouse, they imagine themselves in a heated debate, each side volleying points back and forth trying to "one up" the other person and win the argument. An argument between a husband and a wife is not about who gets the trophy at the end of the night. If you walk away satisfied that you have won the argument, then you've already lost.

Learn to allow your spouse to talk about what's bothering him or her without mentally preparing a comeback. For too many couples it is simply the spouse that is better with crafting words who wins every argument. The other spouse walks away from disagreements over and over again, feeling as if they've been dragged through the mud. Give your spouse the opportunity to speak his or her mind and then the tables will turn and you can do the same in a calm, loving manner.

5. Never give the impression that your spouse is making a big deal out of what he or she is feeling. What's important to your spouse should be important to you.

There is an important step in conflict management called validation. When someone is feeling put down, shut out or unappreciated, they are feeling that way for a reason. Validation is acknowledging that they have a right to feel that way, *even if you disagree.*

If a husband approaches his wife and shares that when she schleps the children off to his arms as soon as he walks in the door, it makes him feel like she is insensitive to the hard day of work he has also had, he needs to know that his wife cares about the way he feels. When a wife shares with her husband that she believes it unfair that he still attends hi bi-weekly basketball league and leaves her alone with the children, the husband needs to listen regardless of whether or not he agrees.

When you bring an issue or concern in front of another person and are met with ridicule and laughter, it can make you feel small and insignificant. Too many times if this continues to happen in a marriage then the spouse on the receiving end will slowly suppress their own needs and wants, becoming a shell of the person they were prior to marriage. Whatever your spouse is feeling should be important and significant.

6. See your marriage as greater than the issue that is creating the conflict.

You would be surprised at the number of conflicts that go unresolved in most marriages. Yes, spouses argue but the argument hardly results in betterment of the relationship. It is possible to argue in such a way that the resolution of the argument actually brings you closer as a couple.

Before this can happen, you must see your marriage as greater than the issue that is creating the conflict. This is not just speaking of the petty day-to-day problems that enter a marriage but is also attesting to the more serious and significant conflicts that arise in any relationship.

Both partners need to be committed to working through whatever life throws at their marriage, be it addictions, infidelity, job loss, etc. While the road is not easy, marriages can make it through extremely difficult situations and couples can rekindle anew the passionate flame of commitment that has been broken. Whatever the conflict is, whether major or minor, both sides must approach the situation committed to maintaining their marriage covenant.

7. Never try to resolve the issue by NOT discussing it. It won't just go away.

Just as many couples fight too unfairly and too often, there are also plenty of couples that hold in all of their anger, bottling it up inside, eventually sweeping it under the rug. Conflict in marriage is like dust in a clean home; no matter how much you rearrange the furniture and the pictures to make things appear neat, the home is still dirty! No matter how much you simply sweep the problems of your marriage under the rug, eventually something comes along to reveal what's hidden underneath.

Conflict avoidance can result in damaging passive aggressive behavior. Each time you choose to ignore a problem or overlook a hurtful situation, it is like you are shaking a can of soda. Eventually the soda will explode under the pressure of the carbonation inside. Married couples that haven't learned to verbally express their anger and frustration are simply biding their time until the explosion comes.

8. Never, ever stay out overnight after an argument. This opens the door for a spirit of separation.

There is a very wise verse in the book of Ephesians

that says:

> *Be angry, and do not sin: do not let*
> *the sun go down on your wrath.*[5]

It is important to realize that the Apostle Paul is not instructing the church in Ephesus to never get angry. Rather, he is acknowledging that there is a way to be angry without letting that anger result in sinful behavior. When that happens, he instructs, be careful to resolve the situation before the day ends.

In the heat of an argument hurtful comments are spoken that open up wounds of insecurities. When this happens, one of the most damaging things that a spouse can do is walk out on their partner, even if just for an evening. The sense of loss that you will leave with your spouse has an immeasurable destructive affect on the relationship. Walking out on an argument is sending a non-verbal sign to your partner that you feel free to abandon ship when things get rough. It ultimately is a cowardly action.

When you and your spouse get into an argument (notice I said *when* not *if*) make a joint commitment to stay physically present with one another until the conflict is resolved. In the absence of the physical presence of your spouse, Satan will take any foothold possible to reinforce the spirit of separation that both of you are already feeling in the midst of the argument. Learn to stay physically committed to the situation.

9. Never bring family or friends into your conflict.

An interesting thing happens when you find yourself

5 Ephesians 4:26

arguing with someone else, be it your spouse, a friend or a co-worker. You tend to seek out others who agree with your side of the argument and use them for backup. People can be very partial and opinionated. When you are in the midst of an argument, it is hard to think rationally and choose an outside person to mediate who will be 100% impartial to both of you.

If you begin bringing others into the argument, your spouse may feel attacked. Essentially you've started down a path that, even if your spouse concedes and admits to being wrong, you have already lost because you've made the game unfair.

This is not to say that sometimes couples do need to seek an impartial third party to help mediate marital problems. It is completely legitimate to seek help when your problems become too big and the hurts become too deep to resolve on your own. Rather than turning to family or friends, seek spiritual counseling from your pastor or clergy or seek professional counseling with a licensed Christian counselor.

10. Be willing to admit that you're wrong for the sake of making things right.

This last principle for resolving conflict is the most important of the ten tips to resolve conflict in a healthy and God-honoring way. First, let's talk about what this does NOT mean. Admitting you are wrong for the sake of making things right does not mean that you offer fake and insincere apologies. You are not offering empty words to simply pacify your spouse.

What you are doing is learning how to be humble.

Humility is willing to forego having your opinion heard. Humility is being willing to let go of the way that you would like things to happen and instead be willing to let someone else call the shots. Humility sincerely desires to serve your spouse above and beyond your own needs and interests.

This aspect of conflict management cannot be overstated and, especially for a Christian couple, true humility comes from looking to and following the example of Christ. Look at Paul's words in the book of Philippians:

> *Let this mind be in you which was also in Christ Jesus, who, being in the form of God, did not consider it robbery to be equal with God, but made Himself of no reputation, taking the form of a bondservant, and coming in the likeness of men. And being found in appearance as a man, He humbled Himself and became obedient to the point of death, even the death of the cross. Therefore God also has highly exalted Him and given Him the name which is above every name, that at the name of Jesus every knee should bow, of those in heaven, and of those on earth, and of those under the earth, and that every tongue should confess that Jesus Christ is Lord, to the glory of God the Father.[6]*

6 Philippians 2:5-11, NKJV

Lest you think that Christ only speaks to your spiritual life, this is a reminder that humility in all of life's relationships, including your marriage, is worth emulating. Christ was more than mere man;

He was the Son of God. He, more than anyone else, had the rights to everything due an earthly king. He could have demanded His way and forced Himself upon people to make them change. However, that was not His way. He came to minister to men and women from a place of humility, mirroring what it means to care of others over the needs of you.

Let the humility of Christ go before, behind and walk in the midst of your marital conflicts.

Chapter 3

I NEED YOU TO UNDERSTAND ME.
(THE ART OF COMMUNICATING)

By the time Bill and Arlene sought help for their marital problems, they were pretty much at the end of their rope. Years of miscommunications and unhealthy arguing had slowly chipped away at their relationship. Honestly, if they weren't arguing about something then they didn't know what to say to one another!

When they sat down and looked across the table at me they both had a desperate, tired look on their face; they were close to giving up. The more they talked through their problems and I more I listened I began to see that Bill and Arlene had never taken time to focus on their communication. Like many couples, they just assumed that this would come naturally in the relationship and when things turned south, neither one considered the way they were talking to each other and failing to listen as the cause for many of their relationship hardships.

"I feel like Bill just doesn't care about my interests," Arlene began.

Bill quickly interrupted and said, "Give me an example of that, Arlene." In return Arlene quickly wilted and slumped back in her chair. She gave me a look as if to say, "See? He doesn't listen."

■ ■ ■

What Bill and Arlene were experiencing in their marriage was a failure to embrace the different ways that men and women communicate. This is not to say that either gender communicates better or more efficiently. That would be sexist. I am simply pointing out what has become obvious over all of my years of pastoral counseling: men and women are different. Not better, not worse, just different.

When men and women are communicating with one another there are some basic principles that will often help the flow of the conversation. Arlene and Bill had never adopted this one very simple philosophy that was literally an epiphany once explained: in most relationships, women think in feeling language and men think in the concrete. Women need to express their emotions and men need specific examples so that they know exactly what to fix. The problem in this, however, lies in the fact that women tend to remember their emotions, the way they felt in a certain situation, much more than the actual words that were said. It can be hard for the two to come together in a meaningful conversation.

In the case of Arlene and Bill, Arlene felt like Bill no longer tried to encourage her in her pursuits. Bill's response of "Give me an example" wasn't meant to demean Arlene or push her feelings aside. He was simply looking for a behavior in his life that needed fixing; he just needed some help in the process of introspection! Women may *feel*, but men need to *know*.

One of the greatest needs of a woman is to communicate her emotions and feelings. Whenever a woman is not able to express her feelings it results in a buildup of emotions and frustrations, which leads to shutting down and disengaging herself from the conflict. Arlene was doing it before my very eyes, leaving Bill even more frustrated. In his opinion, Arlene would simply walk away from conflict and give up as soon as her "feelings got hurt". The truth was Arlene's feelings weren't hurt at all - she simply felt demeaned and shoved aside by Bill's retort.

After removing herself from the conflict a woman's unexpressed feelings will often result in an overflow of tears. Whenever a woman is denied the ability to vent her emotions and vocalize her feelings her tears become the manifestation of the words not spoken. This can cause several problems in the relationship, though. Most men hate to see a woman cry and will do or say whatever it takes to get them to stop. Too many women manipulate their husbands based on a man's emotional response to a woman's tears.

Tears can also be signs of something much deeper. Women tend to avoid conflict in their marriage at all costs. They would rather complain about their husbands to their close circle of friends then actually confront a situation and work through it. Men like to know what's broken so they can fix it. If the toilet isn't working then chances are they will go on YouTube and watch a video, before they call a plumber, on how to fix the problem even if they know they can't solve the problem themselves. They simply like to know what the solution is. They carry this same Mr. Fix-It attitude into relationships.

When a man asks a woman for an example, he is not looking for the woman to justify her feelings. They believe that their wife or partner's feelings have been marooned in some way. Their request for an example is an admission that they don't know anything about fixing feelings but give them a specific situation and they'll try their hardest to never repeat that behavior again. Hopefully, you are starting to see where the miscommunication begins. Women express their feelings, men have no idea what they are doing to make them feel that way, and so they keep doing the damaging behaviors that make a woman feel bad and the cycle continues throughout the marriage.

When we fail to allow one another to communicate our feelings we strip ourselves of the power to heal the relationship. It is important for both men and women to express their feelings. A husband may erupt in anger and yell at his wife, "Stop nagging me!" But that's not as effective as taking a deep breath, looking her in the eyes and saying, "I don't like it when you nag me because it makes me feel like you don't trust me. I will do whatever it is you are asking when I am ready to do it." Men must be willing to communicate feeling language with women.

Conversely, women must be willing to think through specific situations and remember exactly what happened when their feelings were hurt. Imagine if Arlene had said, "I feel like you don't care about my interests, Bill. The other day when I was finishing the baby quilt for our granddaughter, you stormed into the room and asked me why dinner wasn't on the table yet. Couldn't you see that I was busy doing something important to me?" In this scenario, Arlene identified the source behind her hurt feelings. Bill now has a behavior to modify, a problem to solve. He has a concrete category to place the emotions and feelings that Arlene has expressed.

Remember communication is a dialogue not a monologue. Every relationship needs the commitment from both partners to effectively work through the problematic situation and come to a conclusion that everyone is satisfied with. There cannot be someone who yells and someone who always retreats. Communication cannot occur when one partner has conflict avoidance and simply shuts down in silence or tears whenever the other partner brings even the slightest malfeasance to the table for discussion.

In any form of communication there are two essential parts: a speaker and the listener. In a healthy marriage relationship, these roles are interchangeable, volleying back and forth during a discussion like a ping-pong match. Both partners have the right to be heard and should offer that right to the other by listening well. No spouse has the right to simply confront a spouse in abusive language and then walk away. Intimidation has no place in a healthy marriage.

Let's examine a few principles that are useful as you seek to become a better speaker and a better listener in your marriage relationship. Remember that the goal is to grow in both areas as you seek to improve your relationships.

PRINCIPLES FOR THE SPEAKER

1. Focus on your word choice.

When you are the one speaking, the way that you say things becomes very important. Try to focus on feeling language. For example, you could say to your spouse, "You never help me with the kids!" But all you've done is accused and demeaned. Whenever someone feels attacked, they immediately begin to think about all of the times they did help out with the children and use those times for ammunition. Focus instead on the situation at hand and the way it makes you feel. For example, "You've gone out with the boys to play basketball twice this week. I've been all alone with the kids, finishing dinner, giving them baths and putting them to bed. I'm beginning to feel like the parenting is one-sided. I would rather you stay home tonight."

The truth is that many people can't imagine accomplishing anything in an argument if yelling isn't involved. Isn't the definition of an argument raised voices, hurtful words and regretful phrases? Over and over again I have seem the opposite to be true in healthy marriages. When a marriage is strong, spouses have learned to calmly talk through whatever it is that is causing the problem.

2. Focus on the tone of your voice.

When are you the one speaking, the tone of your voice is important. I can remember a young couple who came to my office for marriage counseling and within ten minutes of discussing the husband had raised his voice to a threatening level and was pointing at his wife. She interrupted him with a desperate, "Stop yelling at me!" To which he replied, "I'm not yelling!" I could tell by the look on his face that he was being honest; he didn't even realize he was yelling.

There has to be a level of self-awareness in any argument when you are the one voicing your concerns. Consider the tone of how you say something. For example, consider the phrase, "It's taken you that long to fix the refrigerator?" Take a few moments to consider what that sounds like when someone says it in disdain as opposed to a spouse who is being empathetic to the situation. Our vocal tones and inflection really can make or break an argument.

3. Focus on the words you are saying.

Finally, when you are the one speaking, the words you use are important. Too many couples enter into an argument, guns blazing and shots firing in all directions. Even the best of communicators can become nonsensical when it comes to the way they interact with their spouse. In our errant nature when tempers flare, our sinful instincts kick in and we know exactly what to say, what buttons to push, to make our spouses explode.

Let's take the same phrase mentioned above: *It's*

taken you that long to fix the refrigerator. Imagine a spouse walking into the situation and saying something a little more empathetic such as, "Wow, you've been working on that so long. It must be frustrating. Can I do anything to help?" It seems so simple and also syrupy sweet but the fact is that the actual words that are used in conversation can set the tone for marital intimacy.

Try to think preemptively the next time you have a legitimate issue in your marriage that needs to be addressed with your spouse. Think about what you will say before you even approach your spouse to talk. Think about the actual words that you will use; even write them out if you have to, to make sure that you do not use hurtful language. When you speak to your spouse remember to speak in a manner that is unobtrusive, a tone that is peaceful and words that are helpful in coming to an effective conclusion.

Now that we've focused on the speaker, let's take a few minutes to discuss what it looks when the tables are turned and you now become the listener while your spouse has the opportunity to respond.

Imagine marriage to be like a successful basketball team. A strong basketball team will focus on their defense as well as their offense. In practice they will run plays that focus on both aspects of the game, knowing that if they sacrifice one area for the other then their entire season will be affected. They want to be just as good at shooting as they are at guarding. Their zone defense should be at the same level as their jump shots. All are important in winning the game.

Parenting also has a similar focus. An effective

parent will not only learn to nurture a hurt child and engage in playful tickling wars, but they will also know when and how to discipline effectively. They quickly realize that too much nurture without discipline is damaging as well as too much discipline without compassionate and caring nurture.

PRINCIPLES FOR THE LISTENER

1. Focus on your posture.

When you are the one listening, your posture is important. Most couples struggle with the concept of effective communication because conflict and indifference often cause you to enter into a defensive posture to protect or defend yourself from what you see as an attack on your feelings, emotions or opinions. Crossing your arms, looking down at the floor or balling your fists are all signs that you are in defensive mode and have closed yourself off to the possibility of resolution.

When you are listening to your spouse, keep an open posture, one that is free from intimidation. If you are sitting at a table then simply folds your hands and look your spouse in the eye, nodding and engaging yourself in what he or she is saying. If you are standing then lean back on the counter or wall, with your hands at your sides, communicating that you are not offended or shutting down.

Remove all distractions from the argument. Turn the TV off, walk away from the computer and let the phone ring. Your spouse needs to know that you are physically engaged in what is happening.

2. Focus on the resolution.

When you are the one listening, listen to resolve not to respond. Have you ever walked away from an argument and said, "Oh, I should have said..." Chances are you were not listening to resolve but simply to respond with the next great comeback! Remember that a discussion in marriage is not a debate; you are not trying to win.

If someone is focusing on responding rather then resolving they are simply listening and waiting for the opportunity to respond defensively to what is being said. It's almost as if they are keeping a tally in their minds of everything the person is saying and how they can prove it to be false. *You think I don't listen to you? Well, let me give you an example of how I do listen and then your argument will crumble.* This form of ineffective listening inflames the conflict by creating the see saw up and down or back and forth, tit for tat dialogue. It creates nothing but ineffective listening.

3. Focus on the truth.

Next, when you are the one listening, be willing and open to hearing things that might hurt your feelings. Both spouses should work at creating an environment where hard to hear truths are spoken in a respectful and honest way. It's not easy to hear your spouse say that you are falling short in an area of your life but while marriage is about love and compassion, it is also about betterment. Spouses are working on helping the other spouse be a better person as a result of their marriage. As each spouse focuses on the other, it can create a truly beautiful union where God is glorified in the results.

The following list can help you and your spouse identify and change unhealthy patterns of ineffective listening:

1. Listening to Respond.

2. Interrupting your mate to defend yourself

3. Being pre-occupied

4. No wanting to hear what is being said

5. Not taking your feelings serious

Effective listening involves listening to hear the heart of your spouse. During times of conflict we can become very emotional when communicating our point of view to our mates. I have discovered that most issues can be quickly resolved by just giving your mate an opportunity to express their feelings. When doing so your mate is vocalizing the things that have created frustrations or have affected them emotionally. Listening to resolve means that you listen and acknowledge your part in the conflict.

The steps toward effective communication will not always be easy, but the rewards are endless. God created all of us with the ability to speak and, in His sovereignty, made language a central part of our lives. Psalm 19:14 is a reminder that what you say is important to God:

Let the words of my mouth and
the meditation of my heart be
acceptable in Your sight, O LORD,
my strength and my Redeemer.

It is easy to read words such as those and forget that they not only apply to our spiritual life but to your relational life as well. Proverbs 25:11 instructs:

A word fitly spoken is like apples
of gold in settings of silver.

Choose words that edify and uplift your spouse. Even if you've never learned how to properly communicate with your spouse, it is never too late to save your marriage. Whether you've been married for five years or fifty years, learning how to improve your communication is not beyond the realm of possibility; it is possible to have a healthy and happy marriage again!

Now that you have worked through some of these areas, use the following worksheet to communicate your heart to your spouse. Ideally, each spouse should take the time to complete the worksheet:

1. Take a moment and write down something about yourself or your feelings that you would really like your mate to understand. Be as honest and specific as possible.

_____
_____
_____
_____
_____
_____
_____
_____
_____

----

2. Spouse response: How will I address this issue moving forward in my marriage?

I have heard my mate's heart concerning this issue and I have made a commitment to do my part to understand my mate's needs and feelings. I will remember this day as a point of change in our marriage.

Spouse's Signature

Date

Chapter 4

THIS THING CALLED LOVE

When Nancy and Kevin approached me one Sunday after a sermon, I admit that I was surprised they asked if I offered marital counseling. Even as the day of their session approached, I couldn't think of a single warning sign I had ever picked up on that something might be wrong in their marriage. Even as we said our opening hellos, I was racking my brain, trying hard to be ahead of the game and prepare for what could possibly be wrong.

"So, it's pretty much like this," Kevin began in his matter-of-fact way, "We just don't love each other anymore. We like each other," he said looking at Nancy for confirmation. She nodded her head, "but we just don't love each other anymore."

"We haven't even slept in the same room for the past five years," Nancy confessed, as calmly as if she was telling me she had just picked up the paper.

"So, what we want to know," said Kevin, "is if God would be mad at us if we called it quits and tried to find happiness with someone else. We just don't see how we could ever love each other again."

What they described to me was a typical marriage. They married out of college, having met in church. Both had similar religious convictions but different career goals. Kevin worked while Nancy stayed at home with the kids, and then Nancy went back to work when the kids grew older. Their life became consumed with basketball games, choir concerts and family church events. They never even thought they had a problem until five years ago when their last child left the nest. They honestly thought they had a good marriage and, because of that, never really put much thought into it.

As I began to ask questions and probe them deeper I began to discover a truth that I've seen happen in so many couples lives. Normally it is not a one-night-stand, an addiction or a long-term affair that breaks apart their marriage. Typically, it is small steps through the years of budgeting, working and child rearing that a couple takes away from each other until those little steps have created a deep chasm between them. Like Nancy and Kevin they may like each other, but they feel like love is no longer in the picture. The children have moved out of the house and they suddenly realize that without the school basketball games and choir concerts to keep them connected, they simply aren't. The more I thought about it I realized that even I had often seen Kevin and Nancy at church but couldn't think of any interaction I had had with both of them together, interacting as a couple. They unconsciously decided years and years ago to put love on the back burner until eventually the flame just burned out.

■　■　■

In our society, love is an interesting word. It's thrown around on billboards, movies, radio ads and junk mail fliers to show the opinion of anything from an oil change to a new roof. People sport t-shirts that proclaim their love for New York City, the Chicago Lyric Opera or even the latest pop singer. On any given day we're told to "love" just about anything.

If we view love from the perspective of Hollywood then

it becomes more infatuation then commitment. The storyline of most romantic comedies follow a similar pattern: boy and girl are introduced as two individuals that have less in common then an orange and a potato chip. Often they are at odds with each other, bantering back and forth, fighting and cursing one another until the day comes that they realize they can't live without each other and wed. We, as viewers, are supposed to believe that they will live happily ever after in marital bliss after such a volatile start.

The downfall of so many Hollywood movies is that they leave viewers titillated in their seats and yet lonely in the bedroom. We watch beautiful men and women flirting in designer clothes and picturesque cities, the romance intentionally oozing from the movie screen. The movie ends and we collect our belongings only to return to mundane lives where we must try with all of our being to feel like we are in love with anything, let alone our spouse.

So, in the midst of all that's messed up about love, where do we even begin to look for answers? Is it possible to even define love or is it an elusive ideal that very few can even understand? Do only the lucky ones really find love? Can a loveless marriage ever rise above the emotionless day-to-day existence and find passion once again? Before we get too deep into the subject let's first try to define one of the deepest, dirtiest and intense little four letter words that exists in the English language: love.

Trying to define love outside the character of God is like trying to learn how to water-ski without ever getting into a boat. It is impossible to define love outside of the triune God.

Love is the revealed character and nature of God's presence in our lives. The bible tells us in 1 John 4:8 *"He who does not love does not know God, for God is love"*. The very essence and nature of God is love. Beyond sovereignty, beyond omniscient, beyond all of the things that make God who he is, we are told in his Word that all of these things begin and flow from his love. This is the origin of love. Without God in this world, then love would not even exist.

God's love is of a different breed then the rest of us. It is wider, farther and deeper then most of us can ever imagine, forgiving as far as the east is from the west. It is God's love that sent Jesus Christ, his son, into this world to take the sins of all humankind on his shoulders and offer forgiveness to the world.

For God so loved the world that He gave
His only begotten Son, that whoever
believes in Him should not perish but
have everlasting life. – John 3:16

His love is unselfish. Even someone who doesn't have a deep faith in God will usually acknowledge that God is free to do whatever he wants. God could speak the word and the world as we know it would cease to exist. At his bidding, the winds are stayed, the planets stay aligned in orbit and the sun sets each day followed by the rising of the moon. Even a divine being as powerful as this, however, chooses to selfishly lay aside what he could do as God and graciously showers compassion and mercy on the world. God loves us and expects nothing in return.

God's love is also free. There is not price tag on the love of God. We can never work hard enough to earn it nor have we done anything to deserve it. The Bible is very clear that God's love is a free gift given to anyone who believes in Him.

For by grace you have been saved
through faith, and that not of
yourselves; it is the gift of God,
not of works, lest anyone should
boast. – Ephesians 2:8-9

God's love brings freedom to all those that believe in Him and embrace the love that He gives. Loving God, similar to a healthy marriage, is not an old ball-and-chain of religion around a believer's life. Quite the contrary, God's love frees you and I to do and be more than we could ever possibly imagine. Our lives are freed from selfish pursuits and have now entered a story of meaning and purpose beyond mere human satisfaction. His love gives you wings to achieve and do more than you thought possible because you know God has your back, is with you and cares about the outcome.

God's love is sacrificial. It cost something to love humankind. It cost him his son, Jesus Christ. God looked on humanity and his compassion was stirred. He did not leave us alone to figure out a way to Him, rather, he sent His Son to pave the way for us. When Christ rose from the grave and ascended to heaven, God's love did not cease working. He also sent the Holy Spirit, the Comforter, to be with us, always reminding us and encouraging us in the love of God. As believers, we are saturated in the love of God.

The list of God's love could go on and on as we seek to come to a meaningful definition. In summary, perhaps we could say that God's love is simply perfect. He loves us with the embodiment of what love is supposed to be. There are aspects of it we can understand such as when you have children you can understand the love of God the Father he has for us as his children. And then there are parts of the love of God that we will never understand this side of heaven. None of us, by God's grace, will experience the sacrifice of our children for the salvation of all.

It is important to understand the love of God in the context of your marriage because you are to mirror this kind of love to our spouse and others. When you place the covenant love of God beside the infatuation induced romanticism of our culture, the latter pales in comparison. The love you are to show your spouse is unselfish, free and sacrificial. It is only when you choose to love your spouse the way that Christ loves us, the church, that you can begin to renew an old flame that has slowly died.

Because of this, as Christians, if we fail to allow ourselves to be a point of transfer for God's love then we cannot really proclaim that we know Him. We are meant to display the character of God here on earth for those who do not know God to witness. Through the testimony of love and grace in our lives, we display the power of God's love to the world and, most importantly, our spouse.

Just as God has not left alone with the absence of the physical presence of Christ be giving us the Spirit of God, so, too, the Spirit works within our marriage as well. This display of Love can only truly be released by the love that is present in ones Spirit. The Holy Spirit is the sole delegator of the nature of God in our lives. As humans we express ourselves via our emotions and feelings. These expressions originate from the spirit that works within us. Therefore the expression and quality of love that a person displays will be based on the condition of their Spirit.

Just as Christians can squelch the spirit of God, so, too, can a married couple squelch this spirit of love within their relationship. Let's look at how this relates to marriage by viewing Nancy and Kevin's situation. They have shown no animosity towards each other but they also have failed to show love. They are almost in a neutral-state in their marriage where the temptation to walk away doesn't even seem wrong anymore. The Spirit of God is unable to speak truth into their lives regarding their marriage because it has been too long since they've listened for his gentle leading.

Hopefully you are beginning to see how love starts with the spiritual aspect. This is why a person can say that they love you but there be no fruit of that love. The fruit (offspring) of love is produced by actions and declared by words. You can't release through your life what you do not have working within your spirit. It can't grow out of you if it hasn't been planted in you. The same is true in our marriage relationships. If you are failing to plant the seeds of love in each other's lives, then you will not reap a deep, rich meaningful loving relationship with your spouse. The Spirit can only nurture the seeds of love that have been sown.

Love is the character and nature of God living inside of you. Consider this verse from Galatians:

> *But the fruit of the Spirit is love,*
> *joy, peace, long-suffering, kindness,*
> *goodness, faithfulness, gentleness,*
> *self-control. – Galatians 5:22*

The fruit of the spirit is the outward manifestation and evidence of God's nature. Notice that the scripture identifies nine distinct attributes but they all are the outward expression of one spirit. These attributes are the character traits of God's spirit that dwells within us. Authentic love will always be accompanied by the character traits of the Holy Spirit. In a healthy marriage, both spouses are equally focused on initiating and building their partner up through these traits.

■ ■ ■

While some reading this may be in the situation of Kevin and Nancy, I also realize that there are others reading these words that have found themselves in a marriage of abuse and harm. Many people have been in relationships in which they've been abused both physically, emotionally and even spiritually by those who claim to be giving love. Individuals that claimed to have loved them have killed both men and woman. The cliché "I love you to death" has often become a reality for those suffering abuse at the hands of this false definition of love.

Love never desires to take life; godly love gives life. Remember it's never love that leads to abuse, but an uncontrolled outburst of emotions. Remember your mate is your mate, not your possession. They are a gift from God that he has given to you from the overflow of his love into your life.

If you find yourself in such a situation, then the best thing for you to do is remove yourself from that situation until your spouse gets help for their abusive behavior and proves him or herself to have transformed and changed. I would urge you to seek help from someone in your life that is trustworthy and can help you seek out a better alternative for you during this time.

For most of us, however, our marriages do not fall into such an extreme category. The question then, for the rest of us, is how do we bring this kind of love back into our marriage? The answer, not surprisingly, begins with Christ.

In order for your marriage to be successful, you must first have a healthy relationship with Christ. Are you living a life that pleases God apart from your spouse? Are you walking in his ways and following his commands? It is important to begin asking yourself the tough questions about your relationship with God and spend time in study and prayer, asking God to change your heart and deepen your relationship with him.

Next, you and your spouse must make a commitment to start making thing right once again in your marriage. The slate of the past is clean and the marriage must be willing to move forward if you are going to make it. You must be willing to forgive each other of past hurts and wrongs and be willing to move forward, even if you can only make a small attempt today, to change your marriage for the better.

The first step in this process is to audibly renew your covenant with your spouse. Your spouse needs to literally hear you say to him or her that you are committed to this covenantal relationship and refuse to walk away. Reassure each other that you will work long and hard, not giving up, until the marriage is healed. There is power in words, especially as many spouses experiencing an emotional divorce have failed in the art of communicating effectively. This conversation can and will be the start of something new and exciting in your marriage.

Next, begin spending time together once again. Love cannot be cultivated in the absence of presence. Schedule time each week that is simply "us" time, either leaving the house if your budget allows or intentionally planning activities after the children have gone to bed that forces you to interact with one another. Learn to enjoy each other's company once again. Set aside the bills that need to be paid, the weekly television shows that you are interested in or the basketball games that are never ending, and simply *be* with your spouse. Learn to love what they love.

The next step is to rebuild the sexual intimacy of your relationship. Do not believe the lie that only men desire sex with their spouse. Both partners need to feel loved and desired sexually by their spouse. Even if you have to schedule this time, which at first can seem unromantic, be intentional about making this happen once again in your relationship. If you sleep in separate bedrooms, then move in with each other once again! If this aspect of the marriage is neglected for too long then it is not surprising for each spouse to find sexual fulfillment elsewhere.

Finally, focus on your spirituality. Begin to experience God together as a couple. Learn to pray together, attend church together and spend time reading God's Word and talking about what you are learning. Do this in a spirit of sincere devotion and dedication, longing to become Disciples of Christ *together*. The goal is for each of you to be deeper in love with Christ because of your marriage relationship. You are each to mirror the love of God to one another. No one is leading while the other follows. Each spouse is given this awesome responsibility.

There is a word of caution when pursuing the spiritual aspect of your relationship. Do not look to this as a pietistic fix-it solution to your marriage. You are not reading the Bible and praying together so that God can fix your spouse. It is not a magic equation that will automatically fix your relationship. Sharing your personal devotional life with your spouse is more about the day-to-day experiences of God in the mundane aspects then it is about the concentrated time that you spend together in holy devotion.

Many couples set up their life and try to fit God into the cracks, wherever he will fit. A healthy marriage begins with God's love at the center, the rest of life orienting itself around Him. You simply can't live your life and hope that God will show up. It must be a conscious decision made in a marriage to put Him first, sacrificing all areas of life that do not fit into His goals and plans for you as a couple.

Perhaps the most biblical thing that can be said about love is that it is a covenant, a commitment. It is not based on the emotions of men and women and it is not something that you can "fall out of " or "lose". Learn to redefine love based on the example of Christ and watch as the wounds of your marriage are healed.

Chapter 5

WHOSE MONEY IS IT ANYWAY?

Beth and Xavier got married out of college and never really had significant money problems to speak of. They had both successfully completed their degrees and were enjoying years of financial security where they really didn't have to worry about too much. The salaried position each one had received after school was more than enough to provide for their basic needs as well as some fun vacations and other luxuries. Money went in and out of their bank accounts without too much thought and they were the lucky few who could pillow their heads at night without having to worry about when and if the month's bills would be paid.

Five years into their marriage, however, something changed. Beth became pregnant with their first child and, even though the baby was eventually born healthy and fine, she was put on bed rest and had to quit her job to focus on their newest addition. When the baby was born the thought of going back to work broke her heart. She just couldn't imagine leaving their son in the care of someone else, even if it was a grandparent, and sacrificing time with him so that they could afford a lifestyle. Xavier reluctantly agreed, trying hard to rely on God for their day-to-day needs.

But as one child turned into another and then into a third, the money problems in the marriage only became worse. All of a sudden the laissez faire attitude with their finances was starting to catch up and they found themselves deep in debt and pointing fingers as to how they got into the mess they were in.

■ ■ ■

Jonelle and Maurice were in a similar situation but they knew exactly how their problems had started. To put it simply, Jonelle was a saver and Maurice was a spender. Jonelle had noticed the carefree way that Maurice handled money when they were dating but she just assumed that once they walked down the aisle and said their vows that he would assume greater financial responsibility.

It was fun to be taken to expensive restaurants and, even though she wondered how he could afford them, she assumed that he was just trying to woo her over. She liked the nice presents that always seemed to show up on her doorstep and was flattered by his constant attention. She always thought that once they were married and he no longer needed to impress her that the spending would lessen. She soon learned however, that it was hard to teach an old dog new tricks.

It wasn't necessarily that Maurice bought a lot of stuff, but rather it was that he had expensive tastes so the things he did buy often came with a hefty price tag. If he wanted new golf clubs he wouldn't settle for second best; he had to have the finest quality. If winter was coming and he needed a new sweater, it had to be 100% wool. It was even to the point that whenever he brought a gift home for Jonelle she couldn't even enjoy it because all she could worry about was how much the unnecessary item had cost.

Maurice also enjoyed buying nice presents for other people as well. If his best friend's birthday came around he would receive a designer watch. For her mother's birthday Maurice had bought her a 100% silk scarf. It was beautiful, she admitted, but hard to enjoy watching her mother dote on it without calculating how many years it would take to pay it off. Their credit card debt was piling up and, from Jonelle's point of view, it was created by needless spending on frivolous, overly expensive items.

■ ■ ■

By the time both of these couples came into my office they were experiencing what has led to the downfall of so many marriages: an inability to agree on financial matters within the marriage. Too many couples naively assume that money will take care of itself only to watch credit scores plummet, stress levels rise and eventually it becomes a chasm between a husband and wife that can be hard to walk across. Something as ridiculous as money has driven too many couples apart.

Because financial aspects of a marriage are such extremely personal topics, let's begin by looking at what the Bible says about money and how it relates to our faith. The Bible is not silent in helping us as Christians gain a godly perspective on money and finances. Here are just a few principles that we can learn from the Bible regarding finances:

1. Money should be respected

Perhaps one of the plainest statements in scripture about money is found in Matthew 6:24, *"No one can serve two masters. Either he will hate the one and love the other, or he will be devoted to the one and despise the other. You cannot serve both God and Money."* This is an important foundation to hold before you begin repairing the damage that inconsistent financial accounting has taken on your marriage.

While it is true that money makes the world around, the overarching truth above that one is that God holds all things in his hands, even the financial aspects of world economies. It is not good to see money as a necessary evil nor is it right to see money as worthless since you can't take any of it with you to the grave. We should not hate money but we should also not love money. What we can do is embrace the

53

reality that to live in this world means you must learn how to effectively handle and respect the money that God has given you. Scripture calls for a balance in this area.

2. Money should be planned

For many people, payday comes and the check is burning a hole in their pocket. They can't get to the bank fast enough to cash it and spend it right away. We've all known people, or perhaps are in the situation ourselves, who live from paycheck to paycheck, barely making ends meet. If we're not careful, we can look at a situation like this and assume that we are not making enough money. Often times, however, the reality is simply that we are not making wise financial decisions with our money.

Proverbs 6:6-8 states, *"Go to the ant, O sluggard, observe her ways and be wise, which, having no chief, officer or ruler, prepares her food in the summer and gathers her provision in the harvest."* It is easy for those without money to look at the rich and mock their uppity lifestyle, using such feelings to mask the jealousy they hold in their hearts. In this passage God is encouraging the sluggard, or the lazy person who is unwilling to work, to look at the ant, an animal that works hard all year for its current needs and also has the sense to save for future famine. Having money in the future takes careful planning now.

3. Money should not be owed

According to a recent online article put out by Fox News, the average American owes $3900 in credit card debt.[7] On average, people carry around $44,000 in debt once you consider mortgages, auto loans and consumer debt in addition to credit cards. For many people, this means that they essentially owe almost an entire year's salary before they have even earned it.

Proverbs 22:7 is crystal clear when it comes to debt. It simply states, *"The rich rules over the poor, and the borrower is the slave of the lender."* Essentially you are slave to whoever holds you in debt be that the credit card company or the bank who holds the mortgage to your house.

While some debt cannot be avoided, (e.g. mortgage payments, student loans, etc.) for many couples the stress arises from unnecessary debt. The Bible is speaking towards debt that is accrued for nonessential items that are purchased before the time is right.

4. Money should not be a distraction

Do you remember the parable of the sower in Luke chapter 8? The story goes something like this: a farmer went out in his field to sow seed and he scattered the seed all around. Some of the seed fell on the path, some fell on the rock, some fell among the thorns and a small percentage fell on the good soil. The disciples ask Jesus to explain the parable and he tells them that the seed sown on the thorns represents people who hear the Word of God yet the worries, riches and pleasures of life keep them from following God. What we learn from the parable is that money can be a distraction.

7 http://www.foxnews.com/us/2010/05/30/americans-dogged-debt-stress-despite-whittling-ious-improved-national-economy/

Spend a few minutes and think on the good things about money. Money can be used to buy food, a delicious gift from God. Money can be used to give to the church where you can physically see God working. Money can be used to provide food, clothing and shelter for the poor. Money, used in the right way, is an incredible blessing from God.

What we see in the parable, however, is that too often money can become a distraction that keeps us from God. Here we go all the way back to human nature where we take a good gift from God and corrupt it, twisting it into something that it was never meant to be. Money was never meant to distract us from God, it was meant to turn us towards God.

5. Money should bring freedom

The word "money" can stir up many emotions in the hearts of men and women. For some of you reading this, you can't stand thinking about money. Perhaps you get a panic attack even considering thinking about it! For others, money is unattainable. No matter how hard you work there just doesn't seem to be enough to go around and you don't seem to have the tools to fix this area of your life and marriage.

But, for a small minority of those reading this, you have embraced money and found freedom in the earning, spending and saving aspects of this crucial worldwide monetary system. Proverbs 19:21 states, *"Many are the plans in a man's heart, but it is the Lord's purpose that prevails."* Men and women who have freedom in the financial aspect of their marriage have fully committed this area to God and use their money wisely, seeking God's will for how to both spend, save and borrow when necessary. They have mastered the art of budgeting, carefully tracking where their money is being spent and wisely saving money for the future.

■ ■ ■

Having said all of that, where do we begin to heal a marriage that has found itself deep in debt, completely at odds with financial matters and seemingly in a hopeless situation? The good news is that there is no issue beyond repair in a marriage, even if it comes with many zeroes at the end!

First, couples must consider that all money is held common in the marriage and each spouse should both know and understand the financial situation of the family. Just as government requires checks and balances to work correctly, so, too, the money books within a marriage should be open wide for both parties to see and provide their input.

First off, this is simply a prudent practice when faced with the reality that life is short and we never know when we will breathe our last. Both husband and wife need to be aware of the finances so that, God forbid something happen to one, the other can step in and resume financial care of the family. Secondly, this provides a necessary accountability. It is hard to squander money on addictions or other sinful behavior if you know your spouse is watching and will notice the money that is taken out of the account or never put in. Finally, this simply solidifies the commitment to equality. If both spouses are equal in the marriage, with neither one lording over the other, then both spouses should have knowledge of the checkbook!

This can be an incredibly hard step, especially if one spouse, usually the husband, has been the supreme entity taking care of the money. It takes a great deal of humility to admit that you have mismanaged money and this only becomes harder the longer you have been married. Proverbs 16:18 reads, *"Pride goes before destruction and a haughty spirit before a fall."* We do good to remember that it is in our most prideful moments that the greatest damage can be done.

It is important to remember that if money has been mismanaged, neither spouse is allowed to place blame. Yes, perhaps the husband was bad at budgeting but the wife is also in the wrong in her complacency in the family's finances. Perhaps it is the wife that has allowed spending beyond the means of the family income but the husband has also failed to share in the oversight of the financial situation. Unless a spouse has sinfully squandered finances, then both parties need to agree that pointing the finger will only be a step back in the process.

Once each spouse is fully aware and understands the financial situation of the household, then both must agree to create a budget together and stick firmly to the budget. I am amazed at how many couples walk into my office with ten, fifteen, twenty-five years of marriage behind them having never had a set budget for their family. They have no idea how much they spend on groceries, gas or entertainment in any given month. They could not tell you where the money has gone because neither husband nor wife has ever taken the time to account for any expenditure. Vacations are taken, new items are purchased and Christmas presents are bought without any financial parameters whatsoever. There was never a "no" when it came to spending money.

No matter how long you have been married, it is never too late to start a budget, however, once you do create the budget, both partners must be fully devoted to keeping their spending within the parameters of the budget. If you are a couple that is used to spending and charging whatever you desire, this can be a very difficult step. What you are essentially doing is fighting against the cultural stream of consumerism and forcing yourself to think through each and every purchase.

For most couples, the best way to stick to a budget is to go back to the old fashioned method of cold, hard cash. Once the cash is gone for the month, then no more spending can happen until the month restarts. Many couples are astonished at how frivolous they have been with their spending as they see the wad of cash completely depleted by the middle of the month.

Do not attempt to revamp your finances on your own. There are wonderful Christian resources online to help you create a budget and achieve financial freedom. Dave Ramsey[8] and Crown Financial Ministries[9] are two reputable organizations to help you get started.

Let's take a few moments and spend some time in consideration of couples that have come upon financial hardships due to the sinful behavior of their spouse. Sadly, this is an all too often played out theme in the lives of Christian men and women. Couples come into my office, the wife in tears as she learns her husband has squandered their life savings by gambling it away. I have even had one man who was selling his children's electronic devices to fuel his gambling addiction. One woman sat in my office pouring out her heart as she told the heartbreaking story of her husband pawning their piano so that he could have more money for the casino. She had to sit down with her son who was an accomplished pianist, and explain why the piano was gone.

I have also had couples come into my office where a spouse has admitted to infidelity and spent thousands of dollars on his or her partner. The faithful spouse woke up one day to total devastation in their marriage, their bank accounts depleted, everything spent by their spouse who was creating a second life apart from their marriage commitment. It is amazing the depths of depravity that we will stoop to when we allow Satan to tip the scales of money in our lives and turn our freedom into

8   www.daveramsey.com
9   www.crown.org

lasciviousness.

If you are in such a situation, while my heart bleeds for you in your pain, I encourage both and you your spouse to seek the help of a spiritual advisor to help you repair and seek accountability. The goal is forgiveness and change and that cannot happen if you walk away and give up.

The answer to the question, whose money is it, is simple: it's God's. James 1:17 states, *"Every good gift and every perfect gift is from above, and comes down from the Father of lights, with whom there is no variation or shadow of turning."* Money is a good gift that is meant to bring freedom and happiness into our lives. Money is what we use to provide for our families. It allows us to travel and see God's creation. Money also is the vehicle by which we can help the poor and needy in our communities. Because money is such a good gift, however, Satan is quick to take that good gift and use it to wreak havoc and destruction in our lives. It is important to keep a strong, spiritual perspective over the financial areas of your lives and marriage.

Take a few moments to sign the following pledge as a husband and wife as you seek to repair and restore the damage done to your marriage because of financial failure.

*We promise to be open and honest
with both each other and God when
it comes to our financial situation.
We promise to not spend selfishly nor
spend above our means. Let us give
to God first, our family second, others
third and save the leftover to spend on
ourselves. We promise to work together
to both create and follow the budget
so we can glorify God in our finances.*

Husband's Signature

Wife's Signature

Date

Chapter 6

REFLECT, REFRAIN AND REFOCUS
(REBUILDING THE MARITAL BOND)

By the time Eric and Shantelle came into my office their marriage was only a shadow of what it had once been. Financial problems and a gambling addiction had left their relationship in ruins and they were simply tired: tired of trying to make things work, tired of forgiving each other and tired of pretending like things were going to get better. Even the fact that they graced my office door was a sign of surrender, of acknowledging that they were at the end of their rope. I got the feeling that they were simply seeing me so that they could say with a free conscious that they had literally tried everything, even God.

Standing before me was a classic example of a couple that while physically together, had emotionally separated long ago. As counseling revealed itself it became clear that the only reason they were together was fear of what their parents would say if they split up. Eric even acknowledged that if their parents were dead, they wouldn't even be together today. For better or worse, both Eric and Shantelle had stayed in the marriage rather than suffer the shame of a failed relationship in the eyes of their parents.

Over the months, however, of meeting with Eric and Shantelle, I began to see that their relationship was far from over. Deep inside each of them, whether they admitted it or not, there was still a spark of love and commitment. I held onto that one spark through the months of counseling this couple, believing that God was not finished with their marriage just yet. Literally before my eyes the transformation was beginning to take place. God began healing their marriage and I had the privilege to watch it happen.

I watched as they worked their way through conflict resolution. They began to realize that, like many couples, the amount of arguments were not the problem. The problem was that no matter how many times they argued, or "discussed loudly" as Shantelle affectionately said, their arguments never accomplished anything. They would simply yell it out, sweep it under the rug and leave the dust festering there for the next outburst when it would be whisked in one another's faces once again.

Slowly they began to talk to one another with dignity, acknowledging that beyond hurting each other with the amount of backlash, they were ultimately hurting the heart of God and distorting the plan that He had for their marriage. Once they began treating each other with respect and communicating effectively, they slowly began to strengthen and grow on this foundation.

Beyond communication during disagreements, however, Eric and Shantelle had simply stopped trying to communicate to one another at all. Somewhere along the line Shantelle had simply pursed her lips to the point of no return and Eric had found solace in work friends and his buddies from the basketball court. They rarely, if ever, spoke to one another about what was going on in their lives, let alone the depths of their heart. Through counseling and humility both Eric and Shantelle learned to talk and listen to one another in a way that restored dignity and care into their marriage.

Perhaps the hardest hurtle for the couple to get over was confessing and acknowledging that they both had a warped view of love. Both Eric and Shantelle had come from situations where, even though their parents lived in the same house, love was as far removed as the separate bedrooms where they slept. Once the high of the dating relationship had ended, the day-to-day romance of the post "I Do's" fizzled like a dying fire. The few embers that might have remained in the beginning had long been stamped out.

As simple as it may seem, Eric and Shantelle slowly learned to love one another again. The goal was not toleration but rather celebration and they really put their heart and soul into rekindling the emotional aspect of their relationship. Once Eric and Shantelle agreed to give the love of Christ another glance, they began to build their relationship on an unselfish, free and sacrificial love, looking at the example of Christ to help them in their dealings with one another.

Finally, together, we focused in on the issue of finances and really started to dig deep into their unhealthy spending habits and Eric's damaging addiction. It was by no means a quick fix, nor was it a 7-step program, but eventually and with care and love, Eric and Shantelle had put the word "divorce" behind them and were committed to their marriage, their family and the vow they had made before God and others so long ago. In short, they were on their way to a healthy beginning, giving each other a second chance, a second shot at getting things right.

■ ■ ■

Hopefully at this point many of you reading this book are steadfastly committed to rebuilding the marriage bond. Marriage is not for the faint-hearted. It is not for the selfish. It is not for the immature. Marriage will test and try your patience, your character and your commitment to God and others. There are moments with your spouse that will make you weep tears of joy, moments when you will hold one another through intense pain and also moments when you will feel like beating the snot out of each other when things get too heavy to handle. Through all of these intense and passionate moments, hold onto the belief that things can always be rebuilt. Cling to the hope that once you emerge from the rebuilding process, then the foundation can be even stronger and more secure than before. It is not beyond the realm of belief to consider a marriage that has been through an emotional divorce can actually emerge to form a God-pleasing relationship.

The final step in rebuilding the marital bond is found in three simple words: reflect, refrain and refocus. As you work towards marital health, strive to allow these three principles to be the guiding force of your marriage: reflect on the love you felt for your spouse when you decided to spend the rest of your life with him or her, refrain from feelings of frustration towards your spouse and refocus on your marriage by recommitting yourself to the marriage. Use these three principles as guides, working on each one every day to create a healthy marriage that pleases God.

REFLECT

I can remember the moment when I looked at my future wife and it was like a light bulb turned on in my brain. I had a "duh" moment when I realized that this beautiful woman standing before me was the capitulation of everything I had ever imagined in a spouse. She was my dream. She was my treasure. She was the woman for me.

At this moment in time, you can imagine how little effort there was on my part in keeping that feeling alive. I was, in a healthy way, infatuated with my wife. She could do no wrong and there was nothing too difficult or too inconvenient for me to do for her as we continued courting and eventually married.

The reality, however, is that years of stressful jobs, financial worries and child rearing can take a toll on a marriage. Looks begin to fade, a few pounds are gained that never seem to go away and the busyness of life can take us in all different directions.

Don't let life push you so hard and so fast that it leaves your marriage in the dust. Take time to reflect upon the emotional rocks of remembrances in your marriage. Remember times of intense attraction and deep physical and sexual pleasure that you experienced together.

Our brains are funny organs. They tend to forget significant memories if they are not exercised. That's why men and women take pictures of significant events because they don't trust their minds to remember the day exactly. They are hoping with a quick flash to capture the moment in its closest reality so that it can be played back accurately when the longing for remembrance comes. A lack of consciously remembering the good things about your marriage will result in unconsciously forgetting.

Tucked away in the Old Testament is a booked called The Song of Solomon. This book is filled with such sensual pictures that young Jewish boys were forbidden to read the book until their hormonal bodies could handle the intense passion held within its pages. In the book the writer says of his beloved:

Behold, you are fair, my love!
Behold, you are fair!
You have dove's eyes behind your veil.
Your hair is like a flock of goats,
Going down from Mount Gilead.
Your teeth are like a flock of shorn sheep
Which have come up from the washing,
Every one of which bears twins,
And none is barren among them.
Your lips are like a strand of scarlet,
And your mouth is lovely.
Your temples behind your veil
Are like a piece of pomegranate.
Your neck is like the tower of David,

> *Built for an armory,*
> *On which hang a thousand bucklers,*
> *All shields of mighty men.*
> *Your two breasts are like two fawns,*
> *Twins of a gazelle,*
> *Which feed among the lilies.*
>
> *Until the day breaks*
> *And the shadows flee away,*
> *I will go my way to the*
> *mountain of myrrh*
> *And to the hill of frankincense.*
> *You are all fair, my love,*
> *And there is no spot in you.*[10]

This is just one of many passages where the young man and woman in the text describe their beloved with such passion and unashamed intimacy that even a modern day reader would blush. It is this level of reflection that will help renew the intimacy that has been lost in your marriage.

Communicate your ongoing love for your spouse in a meaningful way. Perhaps you can write your spouse a letter describing the various levels of attraction. If you are more skillful in your writing you could compose a poem or if you are musically inclined you could write your spouse a song, singing praises of what caused the initial attraction and pinpointing the current areas that still make your heart flutter.

There is not a love bank in a marriage that reaches its capacity through the years. In a healthy marriage love is constantly being given by one spouse and received by the other, only to have that same love reciprocated. Whether a couple has been married for five months, five years or half a century, there is still a need for reflection and celebration of their love for one another.

10   Song of Solomon 4:1-7, NKJV

REFRAIN

One of the hardest things to do in any relationship is to back off when you are wrong and retreat when you sense that your actions or words have gone too far. I have counseled too many men who get an adrenaline high from cornering their wives and letting them have it and I have seen too many women who get a twisted enjoyment in belittling their husbands. We are sinful men and women and, whether consciously or unconsciously, at various moments in life other people's pain can become our pleasure.

If a marriage is going to heal, there must be space for refrain. Psalm 34:13-15 reads:

> *Keep your tongue from evil,*
> *And your lips from speaking deceit.*
> *Depart from evil and do good;*
> *Seek peace and pursue it.*
> *The eyes of the LORD are*
> *on the righteous,*
> *And His ears are open to their cry.*

The Bible has plenty to say of the tongue. It tells us that the tongue holds the power of life and death[11] and depending on the usage, will either produce good or bad outcomes in our life. The tongue is powerful because once a word is spoken, for better or worse, it can never be taken back. Only in the movies can we turn back time and swallow the words that were once spoken.

I can remember as a child watching the Disney movie Bambi. In the movie there is a character named Thumper, a spunky troublemaker little bunny who befriends Bambi, the young fawn. Thumper has a propensity to say things that, while honest, aren't necessarily tactful. When Thumper sees Bambi for the first time, Bambi has just been born and is still unsteady on

11   Proverbs 18:21

his feet. Thumper blurts out, " He doesn't walk very good, does he?" To which his mother replies, " What did your father tell you this morning?" Thumper looks down at the ground ashamedly and says, " If you can't say something nice...don't say nothing at all." It's amazing the wisdom we can learn from children's films. How many of us could benefit from taking the advice of Thumper and applying it to our marriages!

Proverbs 25:11 poetically reads, *"A word fitly spoken is like apples of gold in settings of silver."* In essence, when words are carefully thought out and come from a heart that desires to heal and not hurt, they can reap beautiful results. It is hard to harbor feelings of frustration towards your spouse and not have those frustrations show forth in bouts of bitter dialogue. It's the old "hold and explode" consequence that happens too often. Bitter feelings simmer inside of us and, like Old Faithful, eventually spring forth, erupting like an uncontrollable geyser. A key step in rebuilding your marriage is learning how to release control and entitlement and humbling submitting to your spouse, allowing the healing hand of Christ to repair and strengthen your relationship.

REFOCUS

Have you ever been to the movie theatre when the projector is first turned on? Before the filler commercials start playing to entice you to the snack bar and the previews start rolling to tempt you back to the establishment to pay for yet another high priced film, there are a few short seconds where the projector is focusing itself, trying to find the best picture quality for the reel of film. When a marriage has been off balance, just like an old fashioned reel-to-reel movie, it needs to spend some time refocusing itself to make the picture clear and readable.

For a marriage, the refocus happens when a couple, together, recommits themselves to the bonds and vows they agreed to many years ago when they stood before God, friends and family in their wedding ceremony. For this to happen there needs to be a physical act of recommitment. It is not enough to merely nod heads as a couple and move on; come up with a creative way to renew and recommit your marriage vows to one another.

Perhaps, if you have the resources, it is time to renew your vows and plan another marriage ceremony of recommitment. In this way you are accountable before others as well as each other to continually work towards marital health.

If finances don't allow for an all-out ceremony then it can be helpful to simply rewrite your wedding vows to one another and speak them aloud in front of trustworthy friends and family that can also keep you accountable. If appropriate, involve your children in this ceremony so that they can see your commitment to making the marriage work once again.

In the Old Testament when God first united himself with the children of Israel, he did so by joining in a covenant with them. Because we are unfamiliar with covenants in our culture, if we're not careful, we can lose the significance of what this one act meant for every single man and woman who would believe in God throughout history. It all began with the covenant of God to a man named Abram:

> *Now the LORD had said to Abram:*
> *"Get out of your country, from your*
> *family and from your father's house,*
> *to a land that I will show you. I will*
> *make you a great nation; I will bless*
> *you and make your name great; and*
> *you shall be a blessing. I will bless*
> *those who bless you, and I will curse*
> *him who curses you; and in you all the*
> *families of the earth shall be blessed."*

God committed himself to His people through Abram. Abram knew that when you enter a covenant with someone it is a binding agreement until death. The purpose of the covenant is to seal the promise. God entered into a covenant with Abram to prove that He would make good on His promises to Abram to bless him and make him into a great nation.

■ ■ ■

Just as a covenant without a ceremony means little, so, too, a covenant without a promise of grace, love and obedience is meaningless. The promise of these three attitudes and actions ensures the successfulness of the covenant. In this way, covenants go beyond emotions, hold fast through difficult seasons and are still binding when physical ailments weaken our bodies. A covenant, by its very nature, is meant to be unbreakable.

As divorce rates continue to climb, chances are there will be fewer and fewer 50th wedding anniversaries to celebrate. Statistics show that marriage rates will continue to drop as more and more young people are choosing to shack up with one another as opposed to going through the trappings of the marriage ceremony. In short, we've come to a point in our society where the covenant of marriage has lost its value and meaning. If you are going to emerge from an emotional divorce then you must regain your belief in the power of the marriage covenant you and your spouse entered into before one another and God.

If we are not careful we can elevate love, idolizing and assigning attributes that God never intended for it to bear. Love is not infatuation. Love is not lust. Love is something much more deeper and more profound. When a man and woman come together as husband and wife something profoundly deep and profoundly spiritual is happening in that union. It is not something to be taken lightly and it is not something to step out of haphazardly.

Starting now, reflect on the covenant that you made with your spouse. Ponder the moments when love was new and fresh and the world was alive in the possibilities of a life together. With this picture in mind, bring dignity to your spouse once again and refrain from castigating one another. Instead, learn to speak words that create beauty and trigger desire within your spouse. Finally, recommit to your marriage in a tangible way that can be set in the calendar as a rock of remembrance. Don't let another day pass wherein you take your spouse for granted, ceasing to thank God, the Giver, for the gift of the man or woman he has graciously placed in your life.

76163034R00046